SAPCOOKBOOK Training Tutorials
MM Inventory Management

Michael M. Martinez

EQUITY PRESS

SAP Training Tutorials: SAP MM Inventory Management: SAPCOOKBOOK Training Tutorials MM Inventory Management (SAPCOOKBOOK SAP Training Resource Manuals)

ISBN 978-1-60332-133-4

Edited by Shana McKibbin

The programs in this book have been included for instructional value only. They have been tested with care but are not guaranteed for any particular purpose. The publisher does not offer any warranties or representations and does not accept any liabilities with respect to the programs.

Trademarks: All trademarks are the property of their respective owners. Equity Press is not associated with any product or vendor mentioned in this book.

Printed in the United States of America

Please visit our website at www.sapcookbook.com

TABLE OF CONTENTS

Introduction to SAPCOOKBOOK Training Tutorials

As the cover of this book states, "SAPCOOKBOOK Training Tutorials are the fastest way to Learn SAP, period." I really believe this is true. The cover continues...

"SAPCOOKBOOK Training Tutorials are designed to help you understand what you need to know to get started working in SAP. Written from the end-user's perspective, SAPCOOKBOOK Training Tutorials provide step-by-step instruction on how to execute the critical transactions in each functional area of SAP. This is not a 1000-page reference manual filled with obscure configuration items that you will never use — this book shows you what people actually do in the SAP system."

Now when you start interviewing and working in SAP, you're going to encounter a peculiar attitude. That is: Welcome to SAP. Now go home! That's the attitude I've come to expect from established SAP professionals, and from SAP itself. Especially when you're like me and don't believe in keeping secrets or overcharging your clients — you'll encounter this attitude at every turn.

So be warned that this book isn't for everyone, and it might even be a little bit dangerous. I say this mostly because I encourage a self-training philosophy that is counter to what many established consultants and SAP professionals believe. And you may have to hide this philosophy from others in the business who are generally a conservative bunch.

Many of the people who won't approve of this book believe that if you want to break into SAP that you should somehow go through what they had to go through in order to get a job. Meaning that they want you to spend a pile of money, and they want you to suffer as they did — grinding away for years learning and studying. Or they want you to get into SAP by luck, which is how they got into the business, and of course we can't rely on luck as a plan for our lives. Of course, if you have lots of money and lots of time — by all means, please devote it all to the study of SAP.

But most of all, I believe that established professionals in SAP will not like this book because they want to keep you out of SAP. They don't want any more competition, and so I fully expect this book to draw criticism and negative reviews from people who think I'm trying to give away their secrets. Well, I don't believe in secrets – not in the age of information.

I think that this old way of thinking about a career in SAP just isn't realistic. Because formal training in SAP is expensive, time consuming, there are no secrets anymore, and my core philosophy is that spending time and money to learn skills before you put them into use is risky.

Another component of my philosophy is that I believe that large companies have broken the contract of employment – individuals can no longer rely on businesses to "take care of them" with pensions, perhaps as our forefathers could. Now companies want you to arrive pre-trained (pushing the training cost to you) with skills that they need (pushing the risk of learning these skills to you) and when they don't need the skill any more, they push you out of the door (saving themselves money).

So since big corporations have broken the contract of employment, I really think it's appropriate for you, the humble worker or employee, to break a contract or two yourself. You don't need to fall in line and do things the old way "just because."

The "flat world" of work and life doesn't just *favor* people who can make themselves temporarily useful to big companies – it *demands* that they can quickly acquire useful skills to meet market demand, and then when the demand for these skills wanes, they must be ready to learn another useful skill set – and put this to work immediately.

So I'm going to make some statements that are guaranteed to upset SAP professionals who have been working in the business their entire careers, who think SAP knowledge is somehow privileged information to be kept to themselves.

So welcome to *Breaking Into SAP*. This book is the culmination of my career in Information Technology, and it's a distillation of my unique experiences in the marketplace, working in the SAP business for about 14 years.

This is a book about how to break into SAP, but then again, I also think the material applies to your entire career in Information Technology and business.

I'm really excited about this book, and the online training program I've developed as a companion to this book. I hope you get as much out of this book as I enjoyed making it — my feeling is that there are far too many formal books out there that distance the reader with difficult language. Books that try to show you all of the configuration or technical matter that is associated with the

SAP software. I don't want this book to be like all those books that end up unread, unutilized, and in the trash bin. Please think of this book as an open conversation between you and me.

I'd like you to think of this book as a philosophy that you can use to guide your learning and your future work.

In this book, I will cover everything you will need to know to be a success in SAP, from how to prepare your resume to how to talk to recruiters. I'll discuss all the things that are necessary to get your foot into the door in SAP, and then I'll show you how to move from a permanent employee to a consultant and then to a contractor — if you so desire.

If you doubt my methods, that's fine — but please acknowledge and understand that I'm professing this path because it is the path I have taken personally. Yes, I have done this myself, and I continue to employ these methods. I do not posses any formal certification or training in SAP, yet I have risen to the highest levels of work (and compensation) in the SAP business. And this is my understanding of the business, and how you can get there. And again, my mantra is "Always be breaking into SAP." You're going to take the steps in this book and apply them over and over in your career.

So again, welcome, and I do hope you enjoy the material we've provided here. We do offer a more comprehensive self-study course that normally accompany this manual — the training includes training video, online system access to a practice SAP system, and you can get this training at www. sapcookbook.com.

OK! With that introduction, let's jump right into it and get to the essentials.

The SAP GUI

Before we begin our SAP Introduction and Basic Navigation discussion, we will have a quick review of the SAP GUI (Graphical User Interface). You will need to have downloaded and installed the SAP Logon software. This tutorial will use SAP Logon 640 software, but you can also use SAP Logon 710 release software. We will log into an **SAP Client.** SAP is a client-based system where you need to enter a three digit number that defines the client. The client is the highest level in SAP.

To begin with, select the **Logon** shortcut icon to start the logon software.

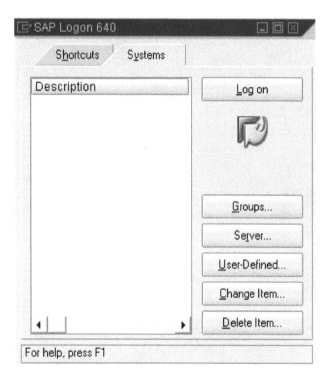

If you just installed the logon software or you don't have the SAP Cookbook server set up yet, you need to enter the server's System Connection Parameters. Select the **User-Defined...** button on the **Logon** screen. If you are using 710, select the **New Item...** button on the **Logon** screen.

For SAP Logon 710 users, the **Create New System Entry** screen comes up. Highlight the **User Specified System** item and select **NEXT**. This is not a concern for 640 users.

On the **System** tab, or the **Connection** tab for 710 users, we enter a **Description**, **Application Server**, **System Number**, and the **System ID** received from SAP Cookbook. Also ensure to toggle the **R/3** radio button.

Access to Live ECC 6.0 IDES Server

Description:	SAP ECC
Application Server:	eccnew.sapaccess.com
SAP routing string:	<leave blank>
System ID:	EC6
System Number:	00
Client:	100

After entering data, select **Add** and your logon software is ready to access the SAP Cookbooks training server. For 710 users, select **OK**, and then **Finish**.

The SAP Logon software is now set up and the SAP Cookbook training server is now available to be logged onto.

Select the **Logon** button and the SAP Cookbook's ECC 6.0 training client **Logon** screen comes up. An SAP system can have multiple clients, such as a Training Client, a Production Client, and Development Client. Each has a unique, three digit identifier. We will work on the ECC 6.0 Client 100.

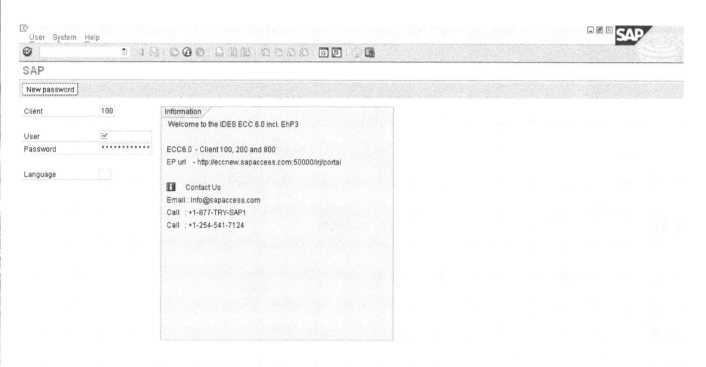

Notice the **User** field has a box with a check mark in it. Whenever you see a field with a box and a check mark, it is a mandatory field. SAP will not complete transactions with incomplete mandatory fields.

SAP Cookbook will have issued you a Username and have set up your password.

Your Username is: _____

Your Password is: _____

After entering the client, your username and your password, select the green check mark 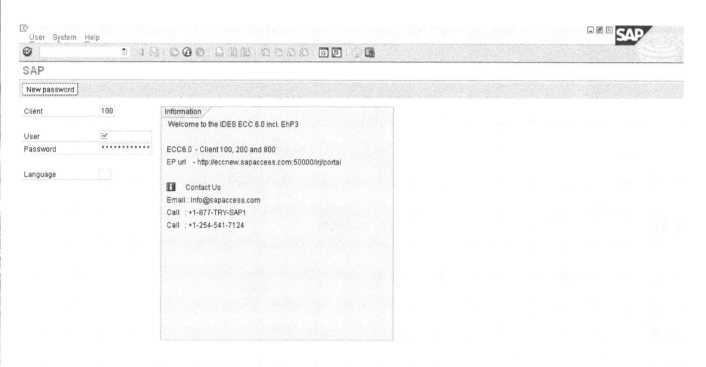, or press **Enter**.

The **SAP Easy Access** screen comes up. From this screen, we can begin all transactions within SAP that we are authorized to perform.

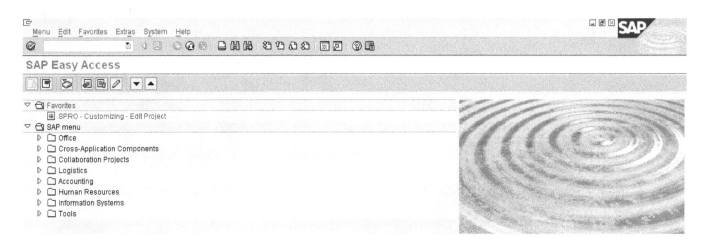

The **SAP Menu Bar** is located across the top of the screen.

This bar changes depending upon the screen you are in, but the **System** and **Help** options are always present. The menu bar provides access to certain transactions and functions.

Below the SAP menu bar is the **SAP Standard Toolbar**.

Notice the **Green Check Mark** icon. Pressing this is the same as pressing **Enter** on your keyboard.

The white field located next to the green check mark icon is the **Command Field**.
Here is where you can enter known **Transaction codes** which are shortcuts to various screens in SAP. There are 16000+ transaction codes in SAP. By entering known transaction codes here, you do not need to navigate the SAP menu tree to find a specific transaction. The **Command Field** can be hidden by clicking on the triangle next to the field.

The **Save** icon is used to save your work or post transactions in SAP.

The **Green Arrow** icon is used to go back one screen, the **Yellow Arrow** is to exit the screen, and the **Red X** is to cancel the current action. ⊙ ⊙ ⊗

The **Printer** icon is for printing and the **Binocular** icons are for searching.

The four **Page** icons with arrows are for paging up and down through a screen. 🔲🔲🔲🔲 You use these to page one screen at a time or all the way to the top or bottom. Some screens can get very lengthy and the use of the search and page features can come in handy.

The **Create Another Session** icon 🔳 is helpful when running multiple transactions.

The **Shortcut Link** icon 🔳 creates a desktop shortcut to the session you're in. This is helpful if you run the same transaction many times throughout the day.

The **Round Question Mark** icon is a help button ⓘ. If you have a question about something in SAP, place your cursor on the field in question and select this icon. Information about that particular field will be shown in a pop-up window.

The **Settings** icon 🔳 allows you to make changes to various screen settings.

Below the SAP standard tool bar is the title bar. It describes the screen you're in (currently, the **SAP Easy Access** screen).

SAP Easy Access

The application bar is next. This row of icons changes throughout SAP as you navigate from transaction to transaction.

The SAP **Menu** icon is handy because it collapses the menu tree completely. As you navigate the tree, many directories will open up and the tree can become cumbersome to maneuver through.

The status bar is located at the bottom left of the screen. All SAP messages, errors and warnings appear here. The information field is located on the bottom right of the screen. Information on the system and transaction codes appear here. The information field can be hidden by clicking on the triangle next to the field.

The **List Detail** icon, is seen throughout SAP. Clicking this icon will display a list of possible selections that are available on a particular window or screen. Click on the icon, select the item **Transaction** and now the transaction codes that you last selected will show up in the information field.

IMPORTANT: Ensure that the technical names can be seen in the directories. On the menu bar select **Extras > Settings** and check the **Display technical names** box, and then press **Enter**. This ensures that we can see the transaction codes.

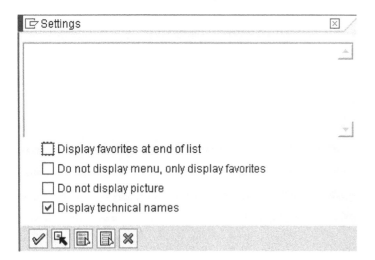

To log off the SAP system, select **System > Log Off** on the menu bar. A warning to save your work comes up before you log off.

Inventory Management

Inventory management is an essential part of the SAP Materials Management system and is critical when it comes to managing costs within an organization. Raw materials that come into a company require the expenditure of capital for their acquisition. The cost of finished goods includes not only require the raw materials to make them, but also the costs of labor, energy, and various additional overhead costs for their manufacture. By controlling, monitoring and maintaining proper inventory levels, an organization can save significant capital by not having it tied to materials in a warehouse.

Often in industry today, we will hear about JIT, or Just-in-Time delivery. This concept is about making goods to order, and not building excessive finished goods inventory or having excessive raw materials inventory on hand. Proper use of SAP inventory management can help reduce the inventory levels on both sides of the manufacturing equation. This is done by producing real time reports on inventory levels and inventory costs, and managing these levels in conjunction with delivery times from vendors and to customers.

In this tutorial, we will discuss the basics of SAP goods receipts, goods movements, and stock overviews. we will also touch on some of the basic inventory information system reports that are available, such as stock reports and coverage reports.

This tutorial will start with creating a simple purchase order so that you can take the order through the inventory management process. It assumes that you understand the SAP purchase requisition and purchase order processing steps required and will not go into purchase requisition and purchase order details.

An important concept in inventory management is Movement Type. Movement types describe the action of moving and receiving inventory throughout an organization and are defined by a three-digit number. There are hundreds of movement types in SAP and movement types can also be user-defined. Some common movement types include:

Movement Type	Description
101	Goods Receipt with Purchase Order
102	Reversal of Goods Receipt
103	Goods Receipt into Blocked Stock
201	EC6 Consumption Reservation
311	Transfer Posting: Stock to Stock
501	Goods Receipt w/o Purchase Order

ME21N Creating a Standard Purchase Order

Objective: To create a Departmental Purchase Order directly and skip the creation of a Purchase Requisition.

To create a standard purchase order, follow the following SAP menu path:

> **Logistics > Materials Management > Purchasing > Purchase Order > Create > ME21N Vendor/Supplying Plant Known**

The **Create Purchase Order** screen comes up. Notice that your personal settings have defaulted into the **Create Purchase Order** screen.

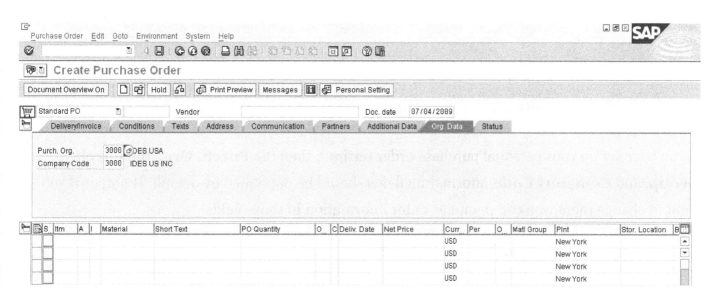

Since we are creating a standard purchase order, ensure that the correct type of purchase order has been selected, in this case a **Standard PO** ![Standard PO icon].

For a standard purchase order, a vendor must be entered. A vendor number must exist for the propose vendor *prior* to creating any purchasing document. In this example, we will enter vendor number **7 Slicks Oil Company**. Vendor | 7 Slicks Oil Company | .

Like a purchase requisition, the purchase order creation screen is divided into three sections, the **Purchase Order Header**, the **Purchase Order Item Overview**, and the **Purchase Order Item Detail** sections. All three sections can be expanded or collapsed by selection of the corresponding section icons .

The Purchase Order Header Section

Expand the header section and select the **Org. Data** tab.

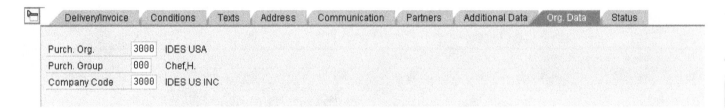

If you have set up your personal purchase order settings, then the **Purch. Org.**, the **Purch. Group**, and **Company Code** information fields should be populated by default. If not, or if you want to change them, you can manually enter information in those fields.

The Purchase Order Item Overview Section

Select the **Item Overview** button to open up a purchase order table where we can enter information about the materials being requested.

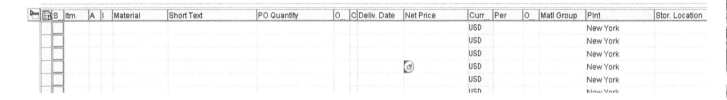

ME21N Creating a Standard Purchase Order

Item Numbering

On the first row of the table, we will enter the first item requested. In the column headed **Itm**, we begin numbering our items. It is suggested that you number items by 10's.

S	Itm	A	I	Material	Short Text	PO Quantity	O	C	Deliv. Date	Net Price	Curr	Per	O	Matl Group	Plnt	Stor. Location	B
	10										USD				New York		
											USD				New York		

Account Assignment

he column headed with **A** is where we enter the account assignment code, which is dependent upon the type of purchase being requested. Use the search function to help you determine which code that you need, as there are about 15 account assignments available. The following list contains the codes you most likely will use:

K – Cost Center

A – Asset

P – Project

F – Internal Order

U – Unknown

For this exercise, we will leave the account assignment blank for simplicity. The addition of an account assignment will require additional data in the **Item Details** section.

S	Itm	A	I	Material	Short Text	PO Quantity	O	C	Deliv. Date	Net Price	Curr	Per	O	Matl Group	Plnt	Stor. Location	B
	10	U									USD				New York		
											USD				New York		

Item Category

The item category information is included in the **I** field. It can be left blank in for our training example. It is used to define how the procurement of the item is controlled; either **Standard**, **Consignment**, **Subcontracting**, etc.

Material

Enter the material number of the requested item in the column headed **Material**. In this case, we want to request the purchase of some motor oil, item 1500-700.

S	Itm	A	I	Material	Short Text	PO Quantity	O	C	Deliv. Date	Net Price	Curr	Per	O	Matl Group	Plnt
	10			1500-700							USD				New York
											USD				New York

Short Text

Here, enter some short text describing the item. Note, however, anything you enter in this field will most likely be overwritten by information from the Material Master or Purchasing Info Record. It's helpful to have something in here as you create the order to help you keep things organized.

S	Itm	A	I	Material	Short Text	PO Quantity	O	C	Deliv. Date	Net Price	Curr	Per	O	Matl Group	Plnt	Stor. Lo
	10			1500-700	10W50						USD				New York	
											USD				New York	
											USD				New York	

Quantity and Units of Measure

Enter the quantity of the material being requested and indicate the units of measure in the **O...Un** field. Ensure that this matches up with the Material Master or an error will appear when you attempt to save the purchase order. Remember when entering a quantity, not to order more than allowed by departmental purchase order rules.

S	Itm	A	I	Material	Short Text	PO Quantity	O	C	Deliv. Date	Net Price	Curr	Per	O	Matl Group	Plnt
	10			1500-700	10W50	100 QT					USD				New York
											USD				New York

Delivery Date Category and Delivery Date

You can use the search function to enter a **Deliv. Date** category, such as **D** for day format, and then use the calendar search function to select an appropriate delivery date. Try to use the vendor's delivery date information whenever possible.

S	Itm	A	I	Material	Short Text	PO Quantity	O	C	Deliv. Date	Net Price	Curr	Per	O	Matl
	10			1500-700	10W50	100 QT	D		12/31/09		USD			
											USD			
											USD			
											USD			

Net Price

The net price is the per unit price. If a purchasing info record exists, the net price will be taken from it. If you enter a price, it will be overwritten if the information record exists.

Plant

SAP will need a plant for the order. If you have set up your personal settings, this should default in. We will use plant 3000, New York.

Storage Location

SAP will need a storage location. This is the ship to address. Use the search feature to help select an appropriate location for the item to be stored.

Now we will go to the last section, the **Item Detail** section. Check the **Delivery Address** tab to verify that the correct address is present.

After entering the data, select the green check to look for errors, and then press **Save** to save the departmental purchase order.

> Standard PO created under the number 4500017315

MIGO Goods Receipt of Purchase Order

Objective: To make a goods receipt to a company's stock while referencing a specific purchase order.

We have created a purchase requisition and in turn created a purchase order from that requisition. After submitting the order to the vendor, the vendor shipped the product to us and we need to receive it into SAP. We do this using transaction code MIGO. **IMPORTANT**: Ensure the company code is available for posting using transaction codes MMRV and MMPV, as described in "SAP Purchase Requisition and Purchase Order Processing".

SAP Menu Path:

> **Logistics > Materials Management > Purchasing >Purchase Order > Follow-On Functions > MIGO - Goods Receipt**

The **Goods Receipt Purchase Order** screen comes up.

If the supplier didn't include the purchase order number on the invoice, then select the binoculars icon to search for it.

The **Good Receipt Purchase Order** pop-up window appears. Here, we enter a vendor and delivery date then select **Find**. We could also enter other data to help us find the correct purchase order number associated with the goods receipt.

A list of purchase orders comes up at the bottom of the screen.

Select the order number, under the **Purch. Doc.** header, and then select the **Adopt** 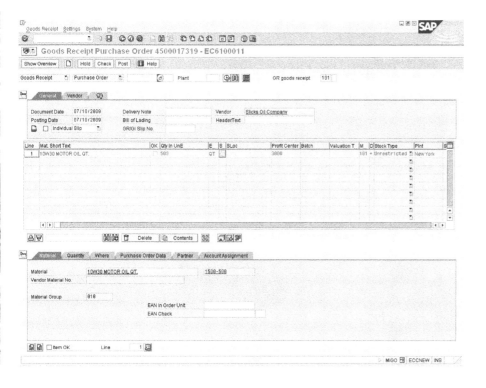 icon. This populates the **Goods Receipt Purchase** order screen. Close the purchase order search results window by selecting **X** icon.

MIGO Goods Receipt of Purchase Order

At the bottom of **Goods Receipt Purchase Order** screen, check the **Item OK** box, assuming you checked over the goods and they appear undamaged.

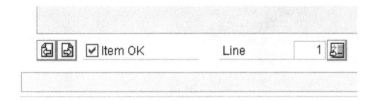

On the item details under the **Where** tab, enter the storage location 0001 for Plant 3000, New York.

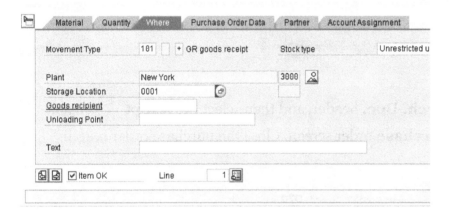

Next, click on the **Check** button ![Hold Check Post] at the top of the screen, and then SAP will verify if the document is OK.

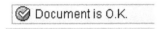

Select the **Save** icon to save the goods receipt, and then SAP will issue a material document number. ✓ Material document 5000012256 posted

Goods Receipt without a Purchase Order

Objective: To make a goods receipt without a purchase order.

IMPORTANT: Ensure a company code is available for posting using transaction codes MMRV and MMPV, as described in "SAP Purchase Requisition and Purchase Order Processing".

SAP Menu Path:

> **Logistics > Materials Management > Inventory Management > Goods Movement > MIGO Goods Movement**

The **Goods Receipt Purchase Order** screen comes up.

In order to make a goods receipt without a purchase order, we need to change the screen layout.

Select the F4 Search function, next to **Purchase Order** field Purchase Order . Click **Other**... and the **Goods Receipt Other** screen layout comes up.

In the item details section, on the **Material** tab, enter the material number. You may need to use the search function to accurately enter the material number if there isn't an appropriate purchase order to use.

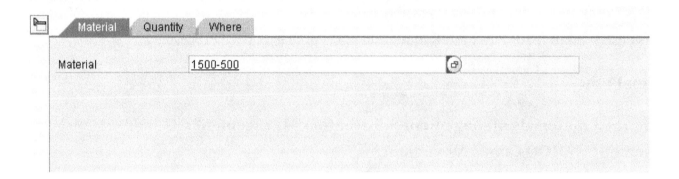

Next, enter the quantity received on the **Quantity** tab.

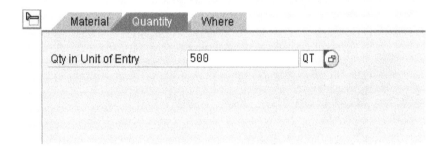

Next, enter the storage location and plant on the **Where** tab, and then click the green check mark or select **Enter**.

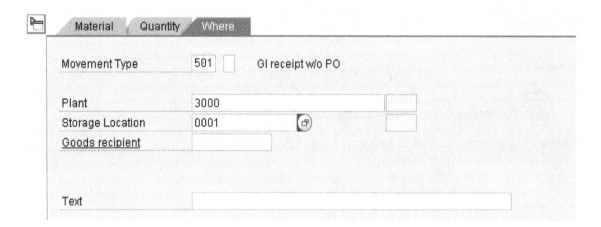

Notice that **Movement Type** 501 (G/I (goods issue) receipt without a purchase order) automatically appears.

Select the green check mark and SAP will look for errors and omissions prior to allowing the posting. SAP will automatically fill in the **Item Overview** section as well.

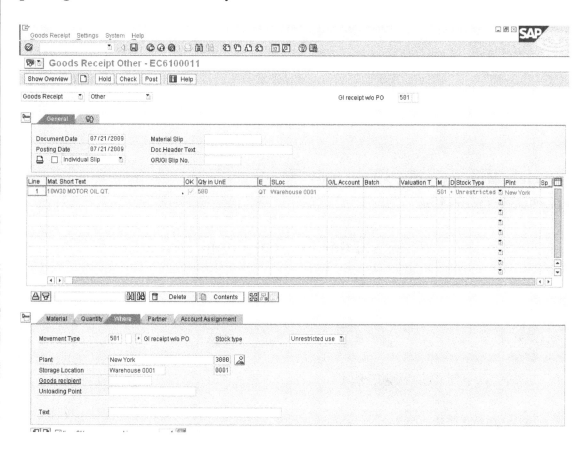

Save the goods receipt by selecting **Save** icon. SAP will post the goods receipt and create a material document number. Inventory should now be increased.

Material document 4900037331 posted

MMBE Stock Overview and Quantity Report

Objective: To generate a Stock Overview Report to see stock quantities and locations.

Since we have made several MIGO-Goods Receipts into SAP and into inventory, let's take a look at our inventory using the MMBE Stock Quantity report.

SAP Menu Path:

> **Logistics > Materials Management > Inventory Management > Environment > Stock > MMBE - Stock Overview**

The **Stock Overview** screen comes up. Enter a **Material**, 1500-500 and a **Plant**, 3000, then select **Execute** .

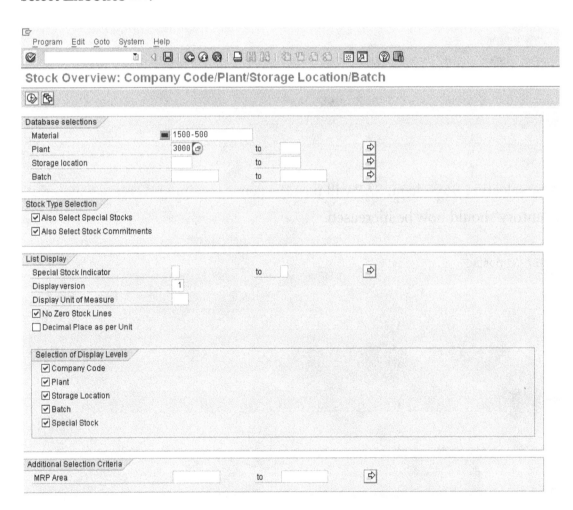

A report of the material entered and the plant where it's located, along with the storage location, comes up.

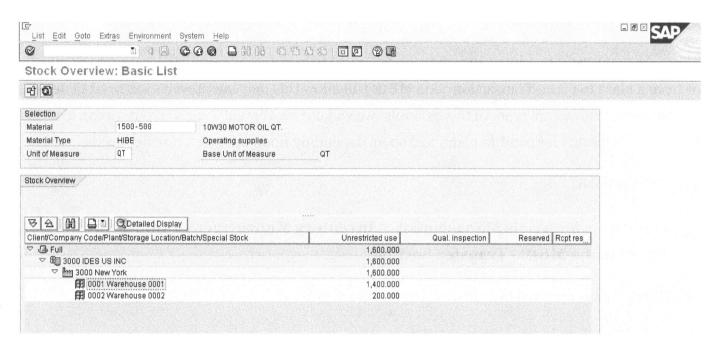

You can view the material movements by highlighting the storage location, and selecting **Environment > Material Movements** from the menu bar. Now, we can see a report of the movement types for the material in this plant's location.

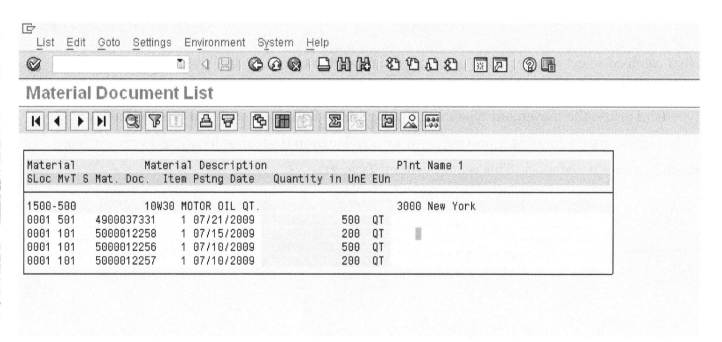

MB1B Transfer Stock to Stock via Transfer Posting

Objective: To transfer material from one storage location to another storage location.

There are many reasons why an organization will need to move stock from one location to another or from a plant to plant. Transaction code MB1B will allow this movement when you need to decide on the correct movement type. In this example, we will use Movement Type 311, but we can also use Movement Type 301 for plant to plant, and so on depending upon our stock transfer needs.

SAP Menu Path:

> **Logistics > Materials Management > Inventory Management > Goods Movement > MB1B - Transfer Posting**

The **Enter Transfer Posting: Initial Screen** comes up.

Next we need select a movement type. Material movements in SAP are governed by movement types. If you don't know the movement type, you can use the F4 search function in the movement type field or use the movement type menu bar option to find the movement type desired. In this example, we are performing a posting from storage location to storage location, as unrestricted stock to unrestricted stock. This is a Movement Type 311.

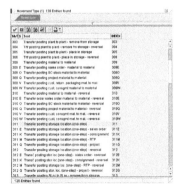

Enter the **Plant**, **Movement Type**, current **Storage Location**, **Reason for Movement**, and then press **Enter**.

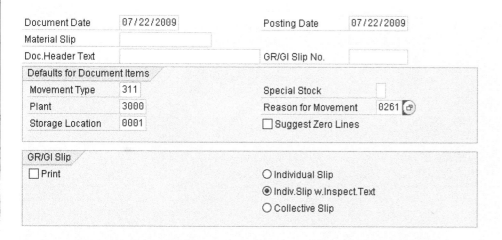

The **Enter Transfer Posting: New Items** screen comes up. Enter the receiving location in the **Rcvg SLoc** field, the **Material**, the **Quantity**, and the **Source Location**. The source location will default in if it was entered on the **Transfer Posting: Initial Screen.**

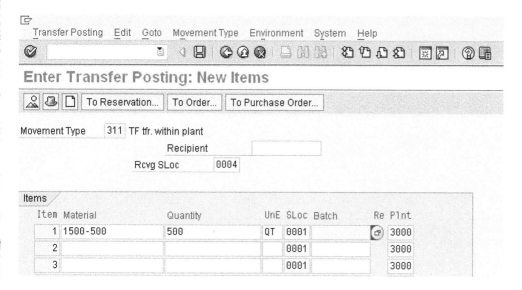

When ready, select the green check mark icon or press **Enter** to check for omissions/errors, then select the save the transfer posting by selecting **Save** icon. SAP will transfer the stock and create a material document number.

Inventory should now have changed at the receiving and source locations. You can view the stock overview of this movement by selecting **Environment> Stock Overview> Stock Material** from the menu bar or by using transaction code MMBE. The **Stock Overview** screen comes up, enter the **Material** number and execute.

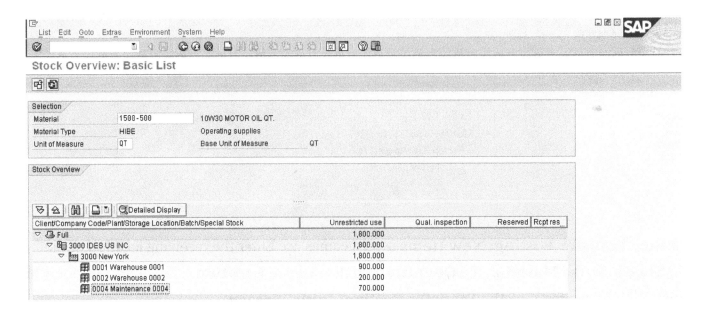

You can view the material movements by highlighting the storage location, and following menu path **Environment > Material Movements**. Now we can see a report of the movement types for the material in this plant's location.

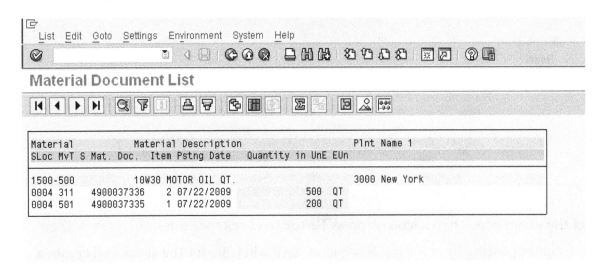

Here you can see that a Movement Type 311 was performed on the 500 quarts of oil.

MB21 Create a Stock Reservation

Objective: To make a stock reservation of a quantity of material. This prevents the use of the material for other projects.

Stock reservation is an important transaction for production planners. With Just-in-Time delivery programs to manage raw material inventory, as well as finished goods, planners need to reserve materials in order to meet their production and delivery schedules.

SAP Menu Path:

Logistics > Materials Management > Inventory Management > Reservation > MB21 - Create

The **Create Reservation: Initial Screen** comes up. Select the reservation **Base date**, let SAP calendar assist, use the F4 search function to select the **Movement Type** (Movement Type 201 is a reservation for future consumption), and finally enter a **Plant**. Select the green check mark.

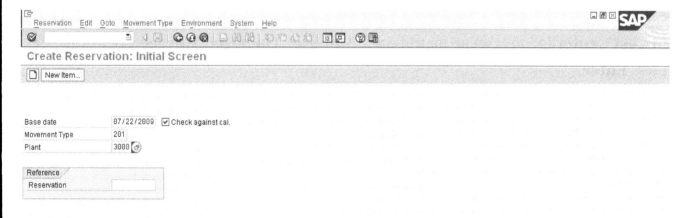

The **Create Reservation: New Items** screen comes up.

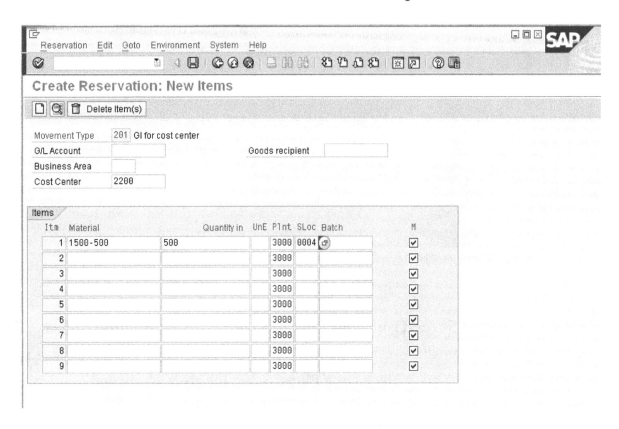

Enter a **Cost Center** (2200 is set up for training), **Material**, **Quantity**, **Storage Location**, and then press **Enter**.

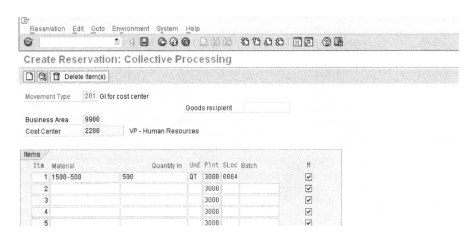

The **Business Area** field is filled by default. The reservation is ready to be saved, but a goods recipient can also be entered if desired. Select the **Save** icon and the reservation is saved. SAP creates a reservation document number. ⊘ Document 0000068376 posted

You can verify the reservation by going to:

SAP Menu Path:

> **Logistics > Materials Management > Inventory Management > Environment > Stock > MMBE Stock Overview**

Enter the material number just reserved and the plant on the **Stock Overview: Basic List** screen. Execute and you should see the material that was just reserved in the **Reserved** column on this screen.

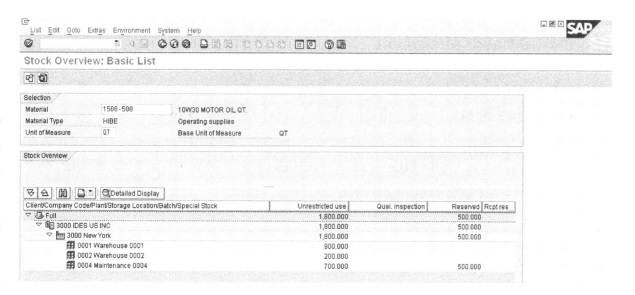

IMPORTANT: While we have reserved the 500 quarts, the unrestricted use hasn't been reduced because we need to issue the material to a cost center.

MIGO Goods Issue to a Cost Center

Objective: To make a goods issue from stock and post the VALUE to a cost center.

Since we have made the reservation of the material to the cost center, now we need to post the value of that material to the cost center. The cost center owns the material and its associated value. This step will also reduce the unrestricted quantity.

SAP Menu Path:

> **Logistics > Materials Management > Inventory Management > Goods Movement > MIGO Goods Movement**

The **Display Material Document** screen comes up. In order to make a goods issue, the screen layout needs to change. Select **Search** in the display box and select **Goods Issue**. The **Goods Issue Reservation** screen comes up, where we can select the search function in the **Reservation** box and select **Other**. The **Goods Issue Other** screen comes up and Movement Type 201 is entered automatically, which is used for goods issued to a cost center.

Now in the **Item Details** section, enter material, quantity, and storage location. Select the green check mark and the **Account Assignment** tab now appears. Enter the cost center receiving the value along with the plant then press **Enter**.

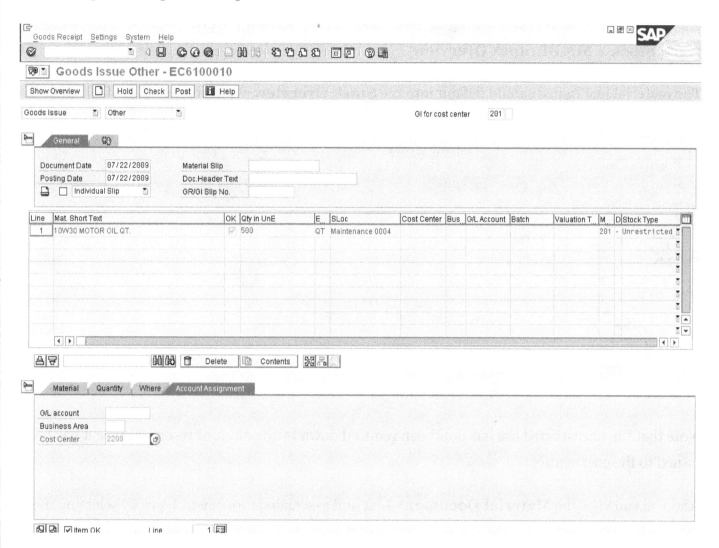

If no errors or omissions appear, SAP will populate the **Item Overview** section. Select the **Save** icon and the **Goods Issue Other** document will be saved and SAP creates a material document number. 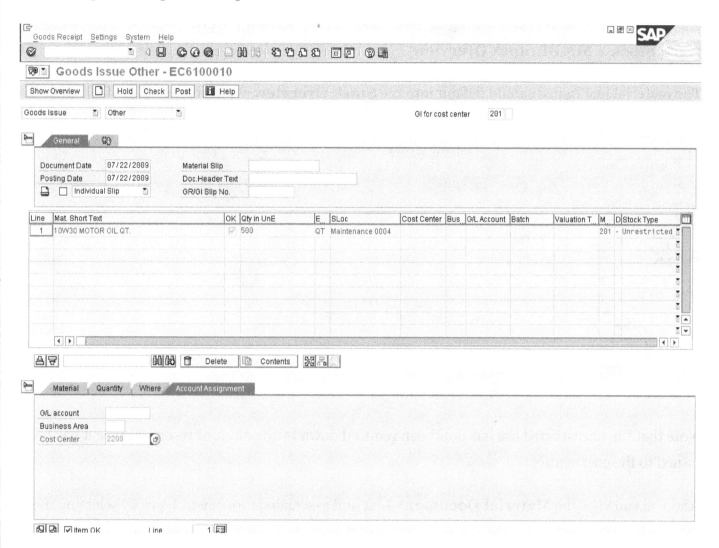 Material document 4900037337 posted

Verify the goods issue by going to:

SAP Menu Path:

> **Logistics > Materials Management > Inventory Management > Environment > Stock > MMBE Stock Overview**

The material just issued should default into the **Stock Overview** screen. Execute.

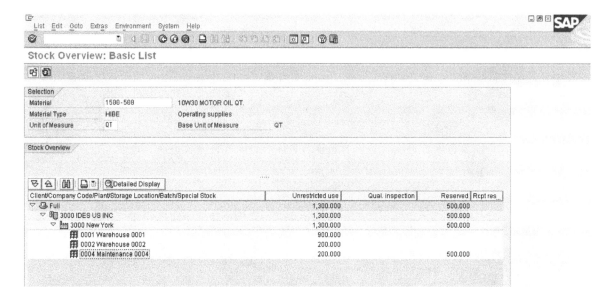

Note that the unrestricted use has now been reduced down by the amount reserved since it has been issued to the cost center.

And you can view the **Material Document List** and associated movement types by selecting the storage location. Then go to the menu bar and select **Environment / Material Movements** and you can see the goods issue document just made on the **Material Document List**.

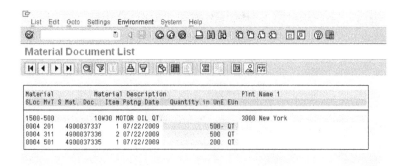

MB03 Display Material Document

Objective: To find an old material document. SAP generates a material document each time there is a stock movement.

SAP Menu Path:

> Logistics > Materials Management > Inventory Management > Material
> Document > MB03 - Display

The **Display Material Document: Initial Screen** comes up. Normally you won't know the material document number, so use the F4 search function to bring up the **Material Document List** selection screen. Here you enter whatever data you have that is related to the material document of choice. Here, we are interested in material documents associated with Material Number 1500-500.

Enter the material number and execute.

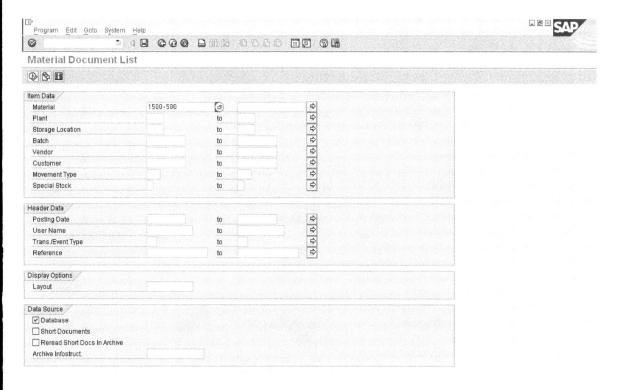

A material document list comes up with all documents related to the material.

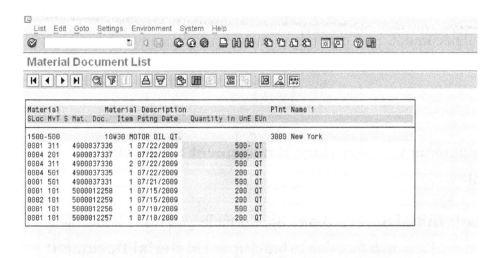

Select document of interest by double clicking on it and note the year. This brings up the **Display Material Document: Initial Screen**. Enter the document year and select the green check mark.

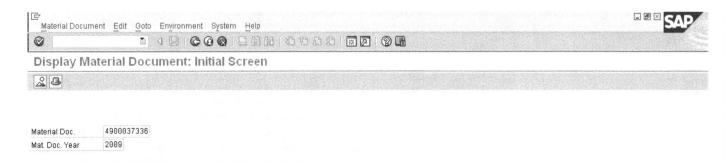

The **Display Material Document** screen is now displayed.

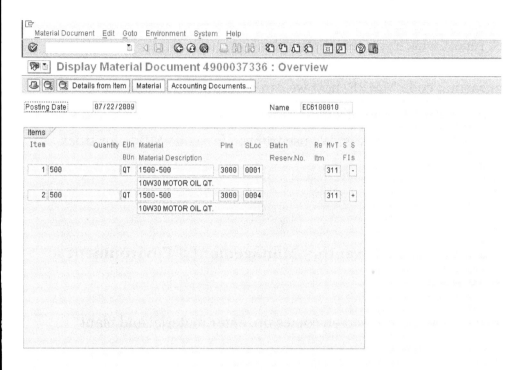

Here you can view the material, the amounts, the movement types and the storage locations. You can also see that there was a reduction of 500 quarts in location 0001 and an increase in 500 quarts in location 0004.

Click on the **Header** icon 🔲 to see header data about the document such as the username responsible for the transaction. Select the **Overview** icon 🔲 to go back to the document.

MB52 Stock Value Report

Objective: To generate a stock report where you can see the stock value.

We have seen earlier, using transaction code MMBE, how we can determine the amount of a particular material is in stock. We can see whether it's in unrestricted use, reserved, etc. Now we want to determine what the value of that inventory is. We use transaction code MB52 for stock values.

SAP Menu Path:

> **Logistics > Materials Management > Inventory Management > Environment > Stock > MB52 Warehouse stock**

The **Display Warehouse Stocks of Material** screen comes up, enter material and plant information, and then execute.

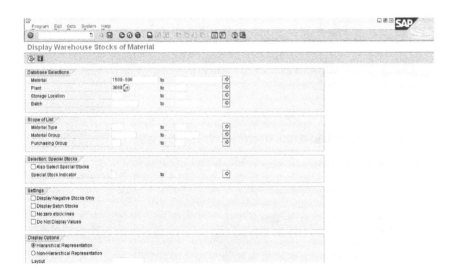

This shows the value of the material available in which plant and at what storage location.

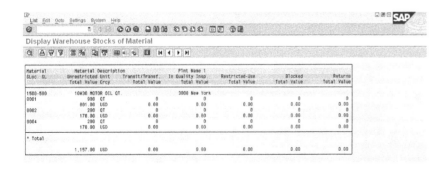

Inventory Management Information System Overview

Objective: To access the Inventory Management Information System and understand the systems layout.

SAP Menu Path:

Information Systems > Logistics > Inventory Management

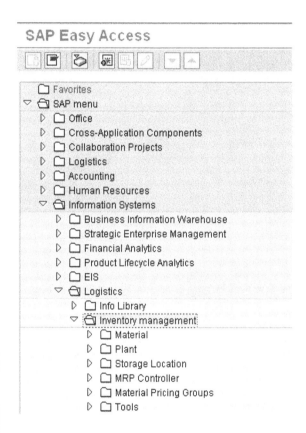

The **Inventory management** reports are structured into six sections:

- Material

- Plant

- Storage Location

- MRP Controller

- Material pricing Groups

- Tools

The first four sections are divided into sub-sections containing specific report analysis subjects which are similar in nature.

For Material:

- Stock (MC.9)
- Receipts/Issues (MC.A)
- Inventory Turnover (MC.B)
- Range of Coverage (MC.C)

For Plant:

- Stock (MC.1)
- Receipts/Issues (MC.2)
- Inventory Turnover (MC.3)
- Range of Coverage (MC.4)

For Storage Location

- Stock (MC.5)
- Receipts/Issues (MC.6)
- Inventory Turnover (MC.7)
- Range of Coverage (MC.8)
- Batches (MCBR)

For MRP Controller

- Stock (MC.D)
- Receipts/Issues (MC.E)
- Inventory Turnover (MC.F)
- Range of Coverage (MC.G)

Now that we have reviewed the location of the **Inventory management** information system, we will review some of the reports in more detail.

MC.9 Material Stock Reports

Can be for Plant, Storage location or MRP controller. See Overview.

Objective: To create an MC.9 Material Stock Report. This report displays stock value, quantity and consignment.

SAP Menu Path:

> **Information Systems > Logistics > Inventory Management > Material > MC.9 – Stock**

The **Material Analysis: Stock: Selection** screen comes up.

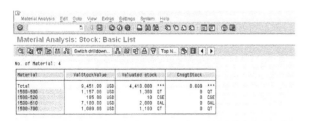

Here we enter which materials, what plants, which storage locations, what reporting period, etc. that we want in the report, and then execute.

A **Material Analysis: Stock: Basic List** screen comes up.

This report displays stock value, quantity and consignment.

Double-click on a material in the list to display detailed values in specific storage locations.

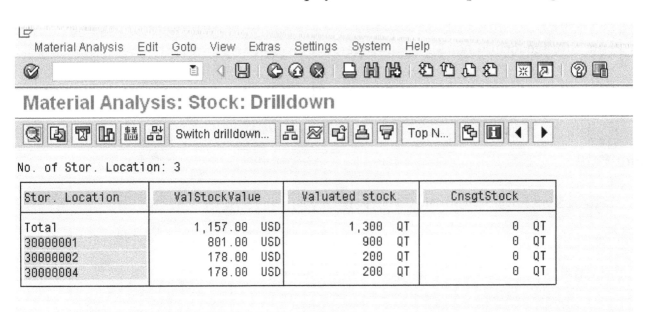

By selecting the **Switch Drilldown** button , you can change the report drilldown structure.

For example, we can look at the report based upon **Material Group**, **Valuation Class**, and so on.

MC.A Material Receipts and Issues Reports

Can be for Plant, Storage location or MRP controller. See Overview.

Objective: To create an MC.A Material Receipts and Issues report. This report displays values of goods received and values of goods issued and the total quantity of material movements related to those values.

SAP Menu Path:

Information Systems > Logistics > Inventory Management > Material > (MC. A) Receipts/issues

The **Material Analysis: Receipts/Issues: Selection** screen comes up.

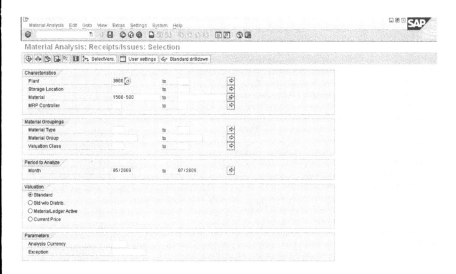

Here we enter which materials, what plants, which storage locations, what reporting period, MRP controllers, etc. that we want in the report, and then execute the request.

The **Material Analysis: Receipts/Issues: Basic List** screen comes up.

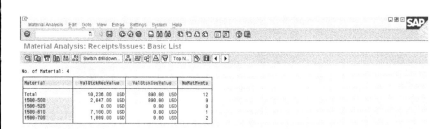

This report shows the value of receipts and the values of issues over a given time period. It also shows the total quantity of material movements which led to the cost of goods received and issued.

MC.B Inventory Turnover Reports

Can be for Plant, Storage location or MRP controller. See Overview.

Objective: To create an MC.B Material Inventory Turnover Report. The report will display inventory turnover for specific materials over a specified time period.

SAP Menu Path:

> **Information Systems > Logistics > Inventory Management > Material > (MC. B) Inventory Turnover**

The **Material Analysis: Inventory Turnover: Selection** screen comes up.

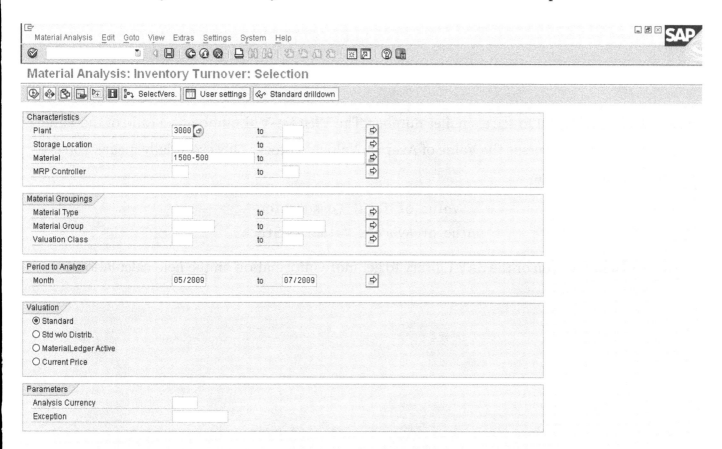

Here we enter which materials, what plants, which storage locations, what reporting period, etc. that we want in the report, and then execute.

The **Material Analysis: Inventory Turnover: Basic List** screen comes up.

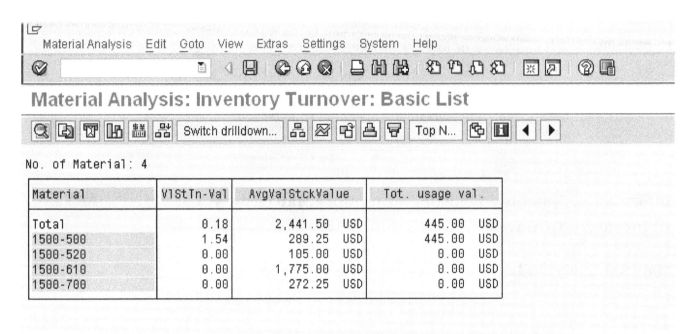

In this display, you want to see a smaller number. The **VlStTn-Val** number is a ratio of the Value of Total Consumption versus the Value of Average Valuated Stock. This essentially means you are carrying a small inventory.

$$\frac{\text{Value of Total Consumption}}{\text{Value of Average Valuated Stock}}$$

Use the F1 Help function or the SAP Library to get more information on the field calculations.

MC.C Material Range of Coverage Reports

Can be for Plant, Storage location or MRP controller. See Overview.

Objective: To create an MC.C Material Range of Coverage Report. The report calculates coverage in days for a particular material over a specified time period.

SAP Menu Path:

> **Information Systems > Logistics > Inventory Management > Material > (MC. C) Range of Coverage**

The **Material Analysis: Range of Coverage: Selection** screen comes up.

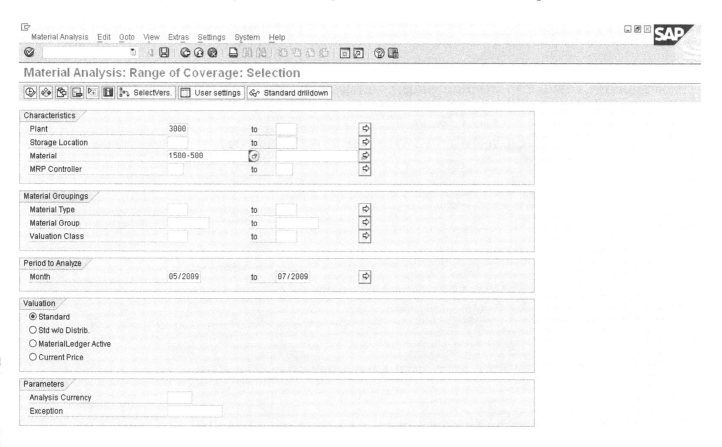

Here we enter which materials, what plants, which storage locations, what reporting period, etc. that we want in the report, and then execute.

The **Material Analysis: Range of Coverage: Basic List** screen comes up.

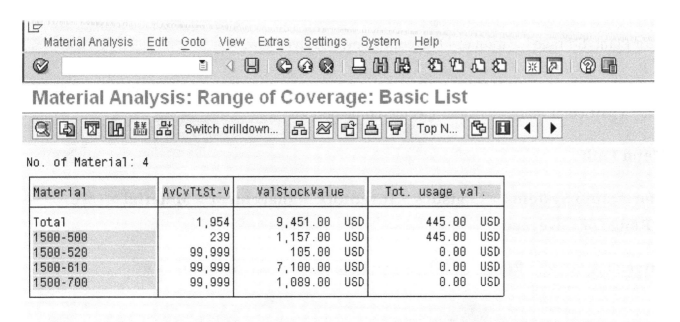

The column **AvCvTtSt-V** shows the average coverage in days for the specified period.

$$\frac{\text{Value of Valuated Stock}}{\text{Value of the Average Total Usage/Day}}$$

MC48 Current Stock Value Report

Objective: To use the MC48 Current Stock Value report. This report shows current stock value by material and can show stock movements and value over time.

In addition to the material inventory management reports previously discussed, which are similar to other directories in inventory management, we will also some additional material reports that can be found in the **Information Systems** menu that concentrate on document evaluations.

SAP Menu Path:

> **Information Systems > Logistics > Inventory Management > Material >**
> **Document Evaluations > Stock Value > MC48 – Current stock**

The **Key Figure: Stock Value** screen comes up. Enter report criteria, and then execute.

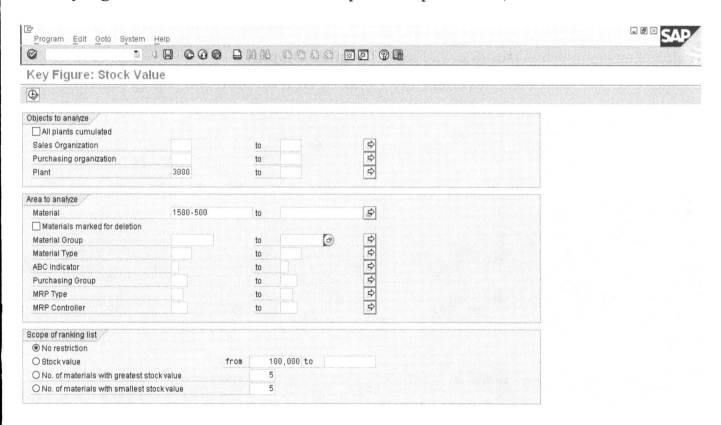

MC48 Current Stock Value Report

The **Key Figure: Stock Value** screen is populated showing the list of materials, their value, and percentage of stock value. This report can be exported, saved, printed, etc.

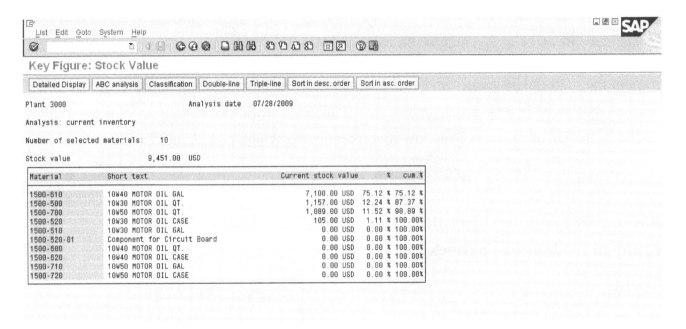

Highlight an item, such as 1500-610, and select **Detailed Display** 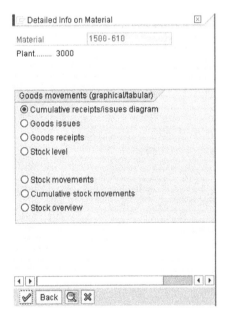 to see additional details on an item. This brings up a **Detailed Info on Material** pop-up window.

From here you can jump to a stock overview list, goods issued or received, stock level, stock movements, and cumulative stock movements. Select the various radio buttons to view specific details. This report can be exported, saved, printed, etc.

MC49 Average Stock Value Report

Objective: To use the MC49 Average stock value report.

SAP Menu Path:

> **Information Systems > Logistics > Inventory Management > Material > Document evaluations > Stock Value > MC49 – Average stock**

The **Key Figure: Average Stock Value** screen comes up. Enter report criteria, and then execute.

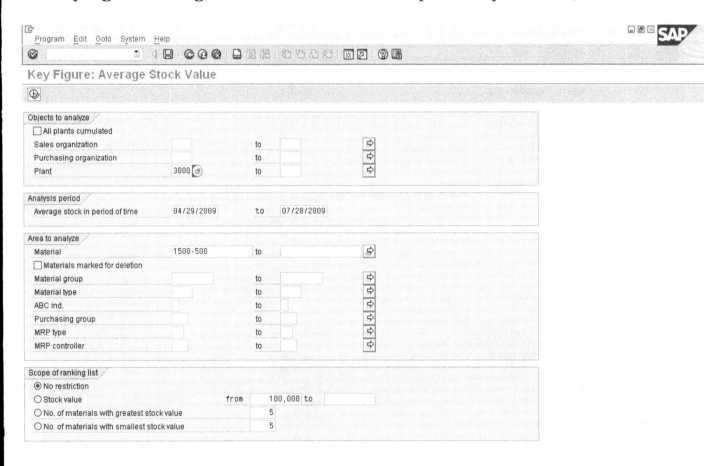

A populated list report comes up on the **Key Figure: Average Stock Value** screen.

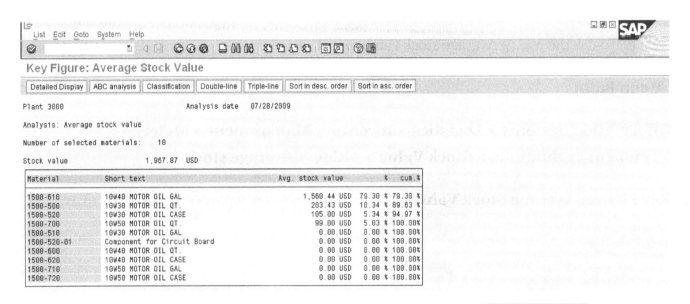

Highlight an item, such as 1500-610, and select **Detailed Display** Detailed Display to see additional details on an item. This brings up a **Detailed Info on Material** pop-up window.

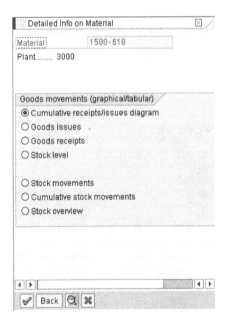

From here you can jump to a stock overview list, goods issued or received, stock level, stock movements, and cumulative stock movements. Select the various radio buttons to view specific details. This report can be exported, saved, printed, etc.

MC42 Stock Coverage Usage Report (PAST)

Objective: To use the MC42 Stock Range of Coverage Usage Report. The report will let you know how long your stock lasts(ed).

SAP Menu Path:

> **Information Systems > Logistics > Inventory Management > Material >**
> **Document evaluations > Stock Value > Range of Coverage > MC42 – By Usage**

The **Key Figure: Range of Coverage Based on Usage Values** screen comes up. Enter criteria, particularly the past **Period to Analyze**. You can select the **Daily Usage** box for daily values in the calculation. This leads to more precise results compared to data from usage statistics, which is often summarized monthly. Execute.

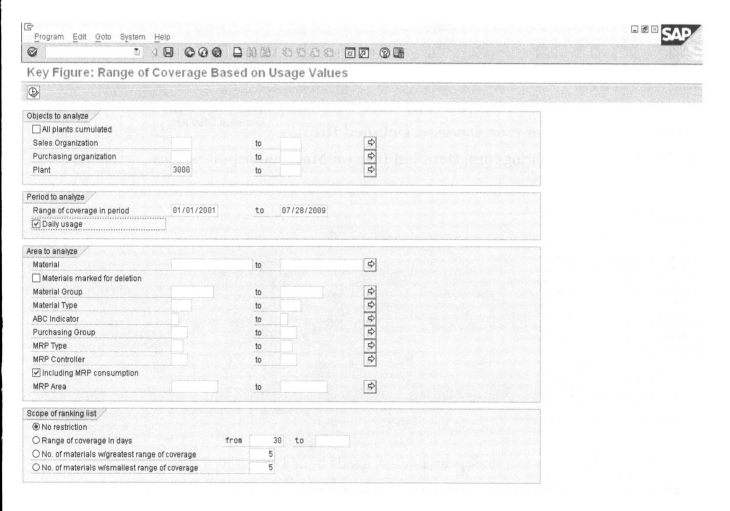

The **Key Figure: Range of Coverage Based on Usage Values** screen comes up, showing the selected criteria.

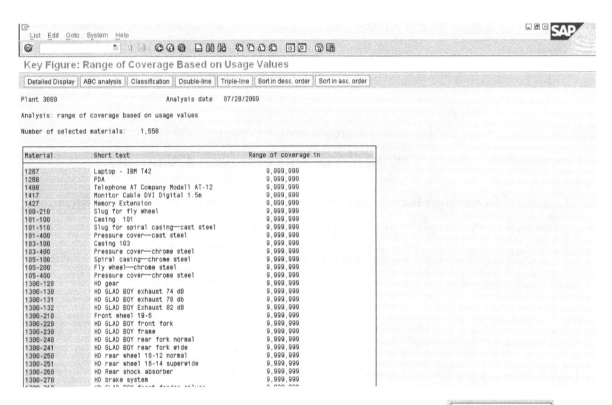

Highlight an item, such as 1267, and select **Detailed Display** ⟨Detailed Display⟩ to see additional details on an item. This brings up a **Detailed Info on Material** pop-up window.

From here you can jump to a stock overview list, goods issued or received, stock level, stock movements, and cumulative stock movements. Select the various radio buttons to view specific details. This report can be exported, saved, printed, etc.

MC43 Stock Coverage Requirement Report (Future)

Objective: To execute the future-based MC43 Range of Coverage Analysis Report. The report will tell you how many days out in the future current material stock will last, based on its planned requirements.

SAP Menu Path:

> **Information Systems > Logistics > Inventory Management > Material > Document evaluations > Stock Value > Range of Coverage > MC43 – By Requirement**

The **Key Figure: Range of Coverage Based on Requirement Values** screen comes up. Make selections, particularly the future period of analysis, and then execute.

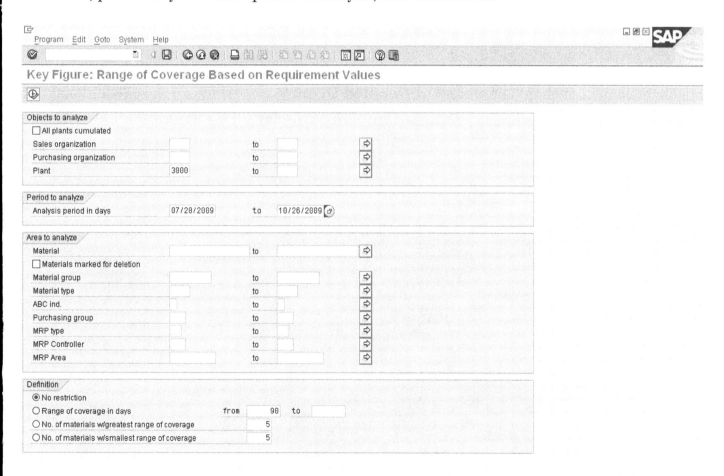

The **Key Figure: Range of Coverage Based on Requirement Values** screen comes up, showing the selected criteria. The range of coverage is in days and is defined as current stock divided by requirements per day.

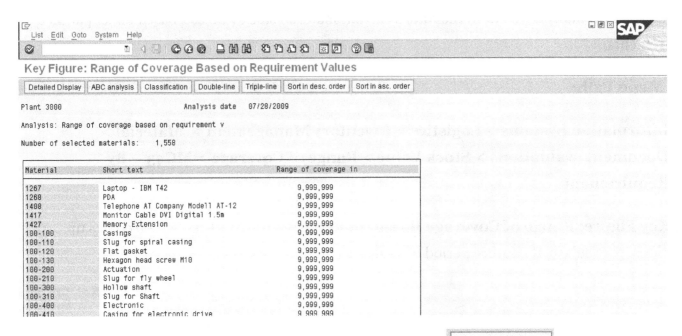

Highlight an item, such as 1267, and select **Detailed Display** Detailed Display to see additional details on an item. This brings up a **Detailed Info on Material** pop-up window.

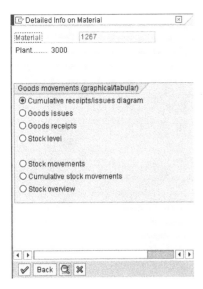

From here you can jump to a stock overview list, goods issued or received, stock level, stock movements, and cumulative stock movements. Select the various radio buttons to view specific details. This report can be exported, saved, printed, etc.

MC50 Dead Stock Report

Objective: To make an MC50 dead stock analysis. This report will identify materials that have inefficient stock amounts.

SAP Menu Path:

> **Information Systems > Logistics > Inventory Management > Material > Document evaluations > MC50 – Dead stock**

The **Key Figure: Dead Stock** screen comes up. Make selections, particularly **Dead stock in a period of time** and **Definition**. In the **Definition** section, you can choose to specify dead stock within a specific value range. You can also choose those materials that have the greatest dead stock. Execute.

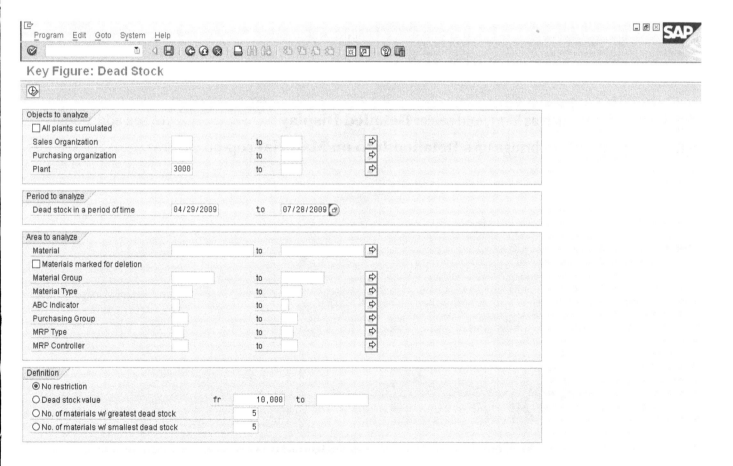

The **Key Figure: Dead Stock** screen comes up with selected criteria, along with **Short text**, **Dead stock value**, and **Percentages**.

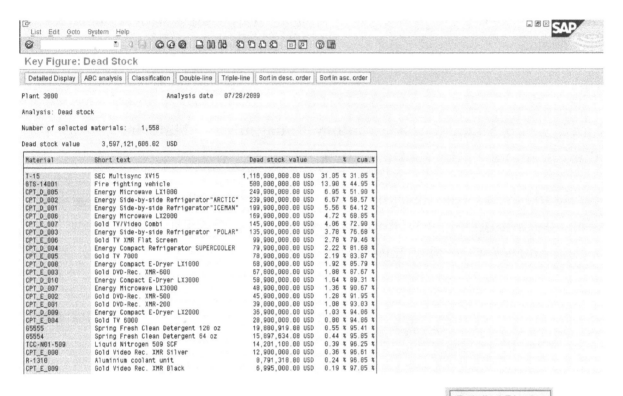

Highlight an item, such as T-15, and select **Detailed Display** Detailed Display to see additional details on an item. This brings up a **Detailed Info on Material** pop-up window.

From here you can jump to a stock overview list, goods issued or received, stock level, stock movements, and cumulative stock movements. Select the various radio buttons to view specific details. This report can be exported, saved, printed, etc.

MC46 Slow Moving Items Report

Objective: To create an MC46 Slow Moving Report. This report will identify days since last consumption for a particular material.

SAP Menu Path:

> **Information Systems > Logistics > Inventory Management > Material > Document evaluations > MC46 – Slow-moving items**

The **Key Figure: Slow-Moving Items** screen comes up. Enter plant and period. Also check the **Daily usage** box. This allows SAP to make the analysis based on actual posting dates and not statistical dates alone. This makes the report more accurate. Execute.

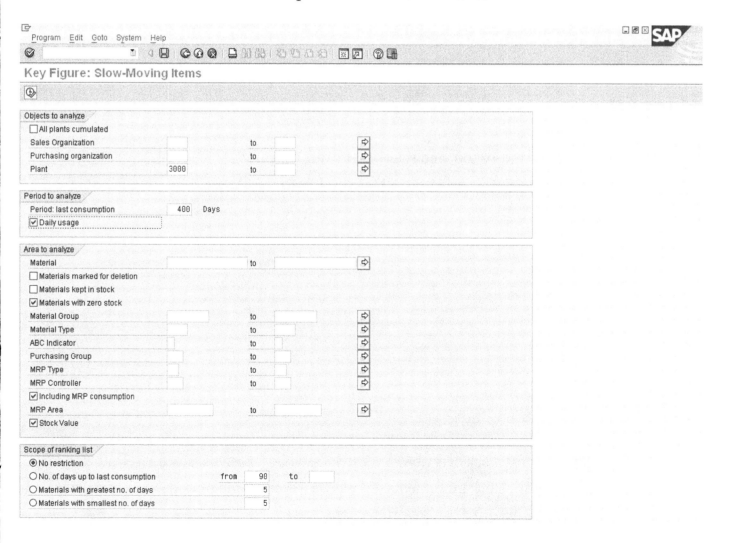

MC46 Slow Moving Items Report

This report shows days since a material was last consumed.

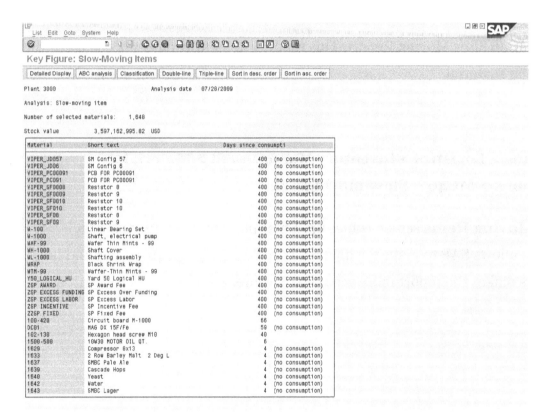

Highlight an item, such as 1500-500, and select **Detailed Display** [Detailed Display] to see additional details on an item. This brings up a **Detailed Info on Material** pop-up window.

From here you can jump to a stock overview list, goods issued or received, stock level, stock movements, and cumulative stock movements. Select the various radio buttons to view specific details. This report can be exported, saved, printed, etc.

MC44 Inventory Turnover Rates Report

Objective: To create an MC44 Inventory Turnover Rates Report. This report will tell you how often average stock has been consumed in a specific period.

SAP Menu Path:

Information Systems > Logistics > Inventory Management > Material > Document evaluations > MC44 – Inventory Turnover

The **Key Figure: Inventory Turnover** selection screen comes up. Enter plant and period, and execute.

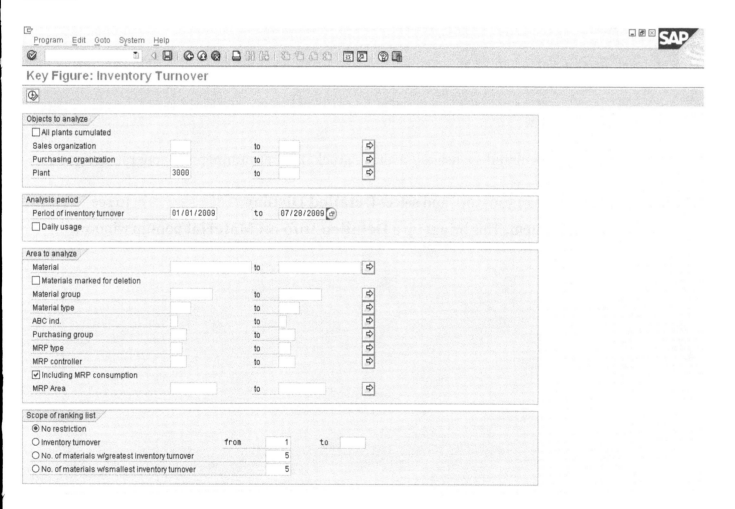

The **Key Figure: Inventory Turnover** screen comes up, showing the selected criteria. The Inventory Turnover report tells you how many times the inventory has turned over in the selected period.

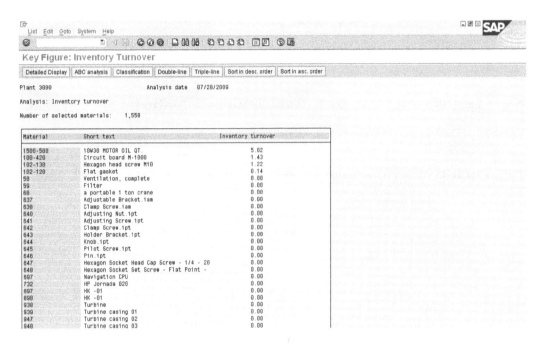

Inventory turnover is calculated as: usage / average stock. Higher numbers, in general, are good.

Highlight an item, such as 1500-500, and select **Detailed Display** [Detailed Display] to see additional details on an item. This brings up a **Detailed Info on Material** pop-up window.

From here you can jump to a stock overview list, goods issued or received, stock level, stock movements, and cumulative stock movements. Select the various radio buttons to view specific details. This report can be exported, saved, printed, etc.

Index

www.ingramcontent.com/pod-product-compliance
Lightning Source LLC
Chambersburg PA
CBHW060206060326
40690CB00018B/4272